Gandhi

by Jill C. Wheeler

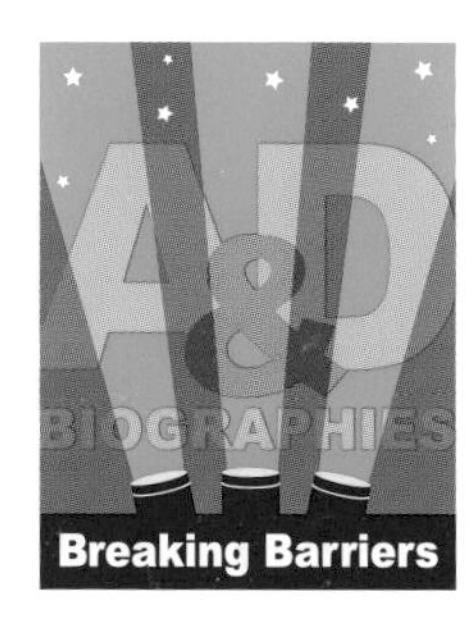

visit us at
www.abdopub.com

Published by ABDO & Daughters, an imprint of ABDO Publishing Company, 4940 Viking Drive, Suite 622, Edina, Minnesota 55435.

Printed in the United States.

Edited by Paul Joseph
Graphic Design: John Hamilton
Cover Design: Mighty Media
Interior Photos: AP/Photo, p. 13, 21, 25, 29, 32, 35, 47, 53, 59
Corbis, p. 1, 5, 7, 8, 10, 14, 17, 18, 22, 26, 31, 37, 38, 41, 42, 44, 49, 50, 55, 57, 60, 61

Library of Congress Cataloging-in-Publication Data

Wheeler, Jill C., 1964-
Gandhi / Jill C. Wheeler.
p. cm. — (Breaking barriers)
Includes index.
Summary: A biography of Mahatma Gandhi, the Indian political and spiritual leader who led his country to freedom from British rule through his policy of nonviolent resistance.
ISBN 1-57765-906-6
1. Gandhi, Mahatma, 1869-1948—Juvenile literature. 2. India—Politics and government—1919-1947—Juvenile literature. 3. Nationalists—India—Biography—Juvenile literature. 4. Statesmen—India—Biography—Juvenile literature. [1. Gandhi, Mahatma, 1869-1948 2. Statesmen. 3. India—Politics and government—1919-1947.] I. Title.

DS481.G3 W54 2003
954.03'5'092—dc21

2002074666

Contents

Peace Remembered

India is home to about 120 million Muslim people and about 1 billion Hindu people. Most of them live together in peace. Yet members of each religion have fought the other for hundreds of years.

The British conquered India in 1858. In 1947, the British government divided India's land into India, which had a large Hindu population, and Pakistan, which was a Muslim nation. As time passed, India and Pakistan continued to fight over land and resources.

The fighting increased in the 1990s. Thousands of people died as Hindu and Muslim extremists battled for territory. In December 2001, the Indian parliament building was attacked. Fifteen people lost their lives.

Many Indians remember a time when Muslims and Hindus worked to live peacefully. Most of all, they remembered the leader who urged all Indians to live in harmony. His name was Mohandas Gandhi. His heroic efforts earned him the title Mahatma, or Great Soul.

Mohandas Gandhi

As homes and stores across India burned from more fighting, many wished Gandhi were with them again. The Mahatma had urged India's Muslims and Hindus to work together for peace. He dedicated his life to making the world a better, more peaceful place.

Shy Student

Mohandas Karamchand Gandhi was born on October 2, 1869, in the seaside town of Porbandar, India. His parents were Karamchand and Putlibai Gandhi. Karamchand had been widowed three times, and Putlibai was his fourth wife. Mohandas had two brothers and three sisters.

Karamchand was loyal to his family and very honest. He taught his children that truth and honesty were important. Though Karamchand had no formal education in politics, he became *dewan*, or chief minister, of the city-state of Rajkot.

Putlibai was a very religious woman. A devout Hindu, she attended temple regularly. She also frequently fasted, or went without eating. Members of some religions fast to express faith. Putlibai also believed in the religion of Jainism. Jainism urges people to be nonviolent, and Hinduism teaches ahimsa, or not to harm other living things. Putlibai taught Mohandas these important lessons.

Mohandas Gandhi as a young man.

A low-caste mother and her two children in India.

Like everyone in India, the Gandhi family belonged to a caste. Castes determined what level of society a family lived in. People were born to a certain caste and could not move into another. People in the same caste had similar jobs, similar amounts of money, and the same religion. And members of one caste were forbidden to spend time with members of other castes.

In India, the castes were divided into four classes, or *varnas*. The top *varna* was the Brahmans. Brahmans were religious leaders and scholars. The second-ranking *varna* was the Kshatriyas. These people were rulers and soldiers. The third-ranking *varna* was the Vaisyas. They were usually farmers, traders, and merchants. The fourth-ranking *varna* was the Sudras. Most Sudras were artists or laborers.

At the very bottom of Indian society were the untouchables. People born into this group had to do the worst of all jobs. They had jobs such as cleaning chamber pots and collecting garbage. They lived in slumbs and could not enter a Hindu temple. People in other castes were forbidden to touch them. That is why people called them the untouchables.

Tourists walk around the ornamental gardens of India's Taj Mahal.

The Gandhi family belonged to the Vaisyas *varna*. However, Karamchand was a political leader rather than a merchant. So the Gandhis had enough money to live well. Unlike many Indians, they had servants. Although his family lived well, Mohandas was still afraid of being teased.

In elementary school, Mohandas was a withdrawn and average student. "I used to be very shy and avoided all company," he said. "My books and my lessons were my sole companions." Mohandas was afraid of being teased by the other students for his small size and ears that stuck out. To avoid other students, he arrived at school just as classes began and left as soon as they were finished. "I literally ran back, because I could not bear to talk to anybody," he said. "I was even afraid lest anyone should poke fun at me."

Like many young people, Mohandas took part in his share of mischief. Hindus are forbidden to eat meat. But Mohandas tried some meat in secret. Another time he stole from his brother. But Mohandas felt bad about his misbehavior and eventually confessed to his father. Karamchand was disappointed, but he did not lash out at Mohandas. This made Mohandas feel worse. It also strengthened the young boy's belief in nonviolence.

Child Bridegroom

In India, parents often arranged marriages for their children. It was common for Indians to marry when they were very young. When Gandhi was 13 years old, he married a young woman named Kasturba. Their wedding was part of a triple wedding, which included the marriages of Gandhi's brother and a cousin. As was customary, the young couple moved in with Gandhi's parents.

Kasturba was a beautiful, strong-willed young woman. Gandhi was a jealous husband and very possessive of her. He forbade her to leave the house without his permission. Kasturba usually ignored Gandhi and did as she pleased. Kasturba had never learned to read or write. And because Gandhi went to school and Kasturba did not, he thought of himself as her teacher.

Gandhi was 16 years old when his father died in 1885. A few weeks later, Gandhi and Kasturba's first child died shortly after birth. Gandhi was sad, but he continued on with his studies. His family expected him to follow in his father's footsteps and go into politics.

Gandhi with his wife Kasturba

A view of London, England.

Gandhi's high school grades had been average. He barely passed the exams to get into the University of Bombay. He went to Samaldas College and struggled with his studies. Gandhi wanted to be a doctor, but his family made it clear that he should become a politician. They wanted him to hold a high office in one of the states of Gujarat.

To accomplish this goal, Gandhi would have to go to London, England, and become a barrister. Gandhi did not like Samaldas College, so he was happy to go study in London. He thought England would be "a land of philosophers and poets, the very centre of civilization." Before he could go, he had to get his mother's permission to leave India.

At first, Gandhi's mother was reluctant to let him go. The family didn't have much money, and they worried. They had heard it was hard for Indians to practice their religion in London, but Gandhi was insistent. His brother raised the necessary money for the journey. Kasturba sold her jewelry to help raise funds. Gandhi had to promise his mother that he would avoid meat and alcohol while in London. In September 1888, Gandhi said good-bye to his family and boarded a ship for England.

Life in London

Gandhi's sea voyage was long and lonely. His English wasn't very good, and he was very shy. So he rarely talked to anyone. He was afraid that the meals served on board had meat in them. He also didn't know how to use a knife or fork. So he stayed in his cabin and ate his own food.

When he arrived in England, Gandhi was wearing a white flannel suit friends had given him. He didn't realize the English custom was that no one wore white after September 1. Gandhi was the only person in a white suit.

London was a frightening place for 19-year-old Gandhi. At first the strange manners, clothes, and customs made him homesick. But he began his lessons at Inner Temple Law School anyway. In order to fit in better, he decided to transform himself into an English gentleman.

Gandhi bought all the fashionable clothes and accessories of an Englishman. He took a room with an English family. He began dance, music, and speaking lessons. In the end, he realized he looked like an Indian trying to be an Englishman. He realized he wasn't being true to himself. After three months of trying to be English, Gandhi decided to just be himself.

A young Mohandas Gandhi, at age 19.

Gandhi meets with European reporters.

Gandhi moved to a one-room apartment and lived alone. He cooked simple meals of bread, cocoa, and boiled spinach. He avoided the bus and walked everywhere instead. Sometimes he walked eight to ten miles (13 to 16 km) a day. He also began studying world religions, including Hinduism, Buddhism, and Christianity. He was captivated by the Hindu concept of giving up material goods to become more spiritual. He was also interested in the Christian concept of turning the other cheek.

At the same time, Gandhi began to learn more about vegetarianism. He had refrained from eating meat because of his religion. Now, he studied other reasons for a vegetarian diet. He joined the London Vegetarian Society and experimented with different types of vegetarian meals. He learned that taste was more in the mind than on the tongue.

Meanwhile, Gandhi continued to study law. He passed his final examinations and became a barrister on June 11, 1891. The next day, he set sail for India. When Gandhi arrived, his brother met him at the dock. He told him that their mother had died while Gandhi was away.

Gandhi had been very close to his mother. Her death was hard on him. And even though he was glad to see Kasturba again, they argued often. So Gandhi concentrated on establishing his law career.

Beginning Barrister

Gandhi began a law practice in his hometown of Rajkot. Yet he had studied law in England. So he knew almost nothing about Indian law. He found that he could not even apply basic legal principles he had learned in London to Indian cases. Indians did not want to hire him to be their barrister. And Gandhi lacked confidence in his skills because of his lack of training in Indian law. He decided to move his practice to Bombay, India.

Business was no better in Bombay. Gandhi's brother referred clients to Gandhi's office. However, in the first and only case he took to court, Gandhi was unable to speak at all. He had to turn the case over to another lawyer and leave the courtroom. He vowed never to return to a courtroom until he could do the job.

Gandhi's brother helped him once again. His brother had heard of a merchant firm that needed a barrister in their South African office. Gandhi jumped at the opportunity to leave India.

Mohandas Gandhi is surrounded by workers from his law office.

Mohandas Gandhi

Once again, Gandhi left India and his wife and two sons behind. He arrived in Durban, in the Natal province of South Africa, in April 1893.

The merchant firm wanted Gandhi to work on a complicated corporate legal case that involved years of financial transactions. Gandhi studied the details of the case. He realized that a lengthy court battle would hurt both parties. He urged them to settle out of court, and they agreed. At last Gandhi had found his calling. "I had learnt the true practice of law," he said. "I had learnt to find out the better side of human nature and to enter men's hearts. I realized that the true function of a lawyer was to unite parties riven asunder."

This realization transformed Gandhi's work. He had never been motivated by money or prestige. Law for the sake of money and power did not inspire him. Law for the sake of helping others did. He soon had all the work he could handle.

A Problem of Class

Like India, South Africa in the late 1800s was part of the British Empire. The country was rigidly segregated. The native black South Africans had no rights under the country's white rulers. Just above blacks on the social scale were people called the coloreds. They were immigrants from Asia and India, and people of racially mixed heritage. Many of the coloreds were Indians who had gone to South Africa to work on British farms.

Shortly after arriving in South Africa, Gandhi experienced the segregation first hand. He had a first-class ticket on a train from Durban to Pretoria. Yet colored people couldn't ride in first class. Railway officials asked Gandhi to go to the third-class section. He refused, so police forced him off the train at the Pietermaritzburg station. The young lawyer had to spend the night shivering in the train station.

This double-deck bus in Johannesburg, South Africa, is marked Slegs vir nie Blankes, *or Non-Europeans Only.*

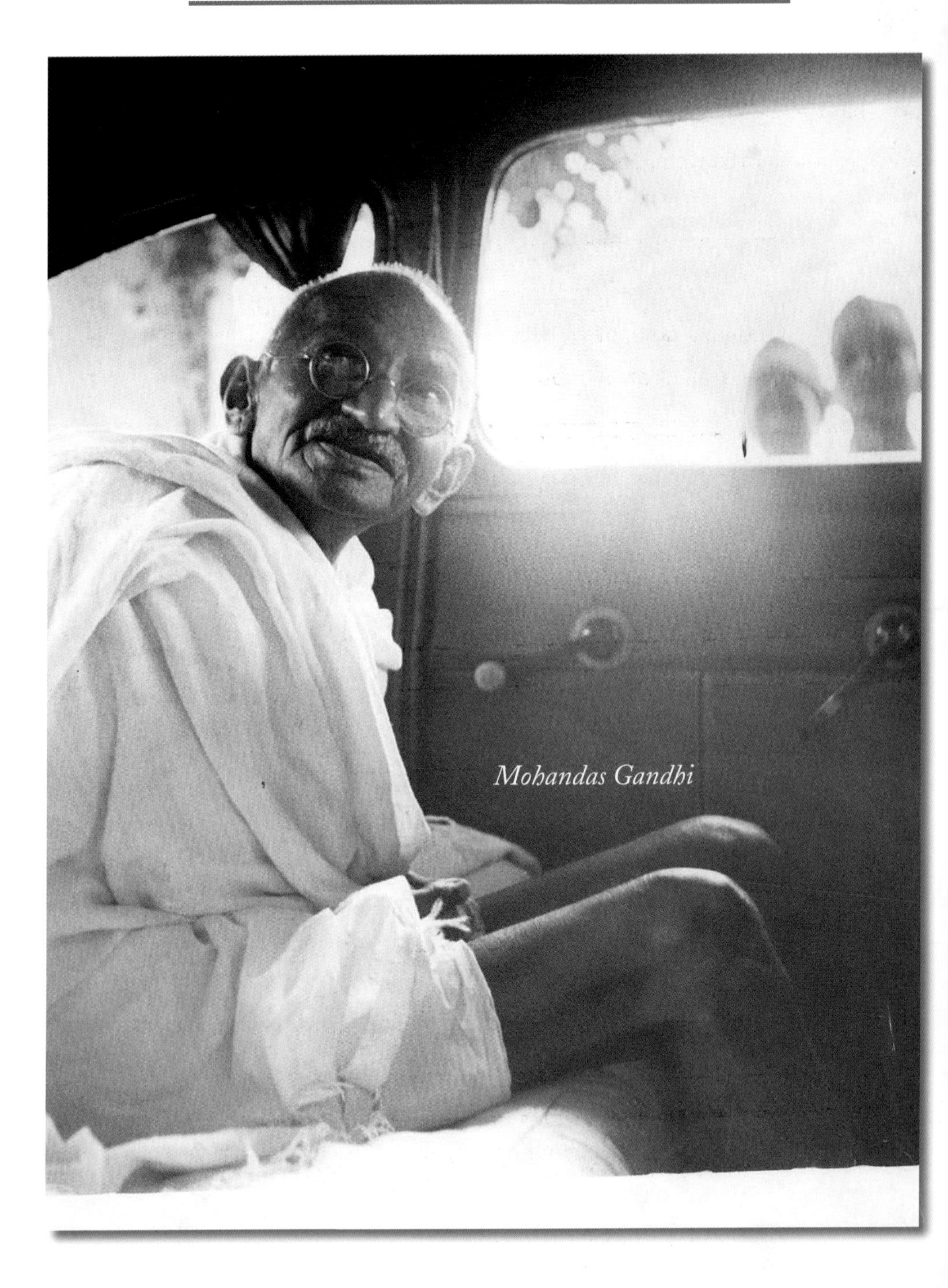

Mohandas Gandhi

This wasn't the only time Gandhi experienced discrimination because of the color of his skin. While he was in South Africa, he was once ordered to remove his turban in a courtroom. He was also forced to sit outside on a stagecoach because dark-skinned passengers weren't allowed inside. He was called a Coolie, a derogatory term for Indian laborers. He was once forced off a public street. Indians, he was told, were not allowed outside after 9 P.M. without a government permit.

During the long night in the Pietermaritzburg train station, Gandhi thought about how he had been treated. He also thought about other Indians who were facing discrimination. Gandhi made a decision that night. He would fight against injustice. However, he would not fight with violence. He would reach people through nonviolent protest and reason. Later, Gandhi called this philosophy satyagraha, or holding onto truth.

Satyagraha would come to symbolize peacefully disobeying unjust laws and rules. It would have its first test in 1894. By then, Gandhi's one-year contract with the law firm was over. He was preparing to return to India when he learned of a pending law. The law would take away Natal Indians' right to vote. Indians in the province asked Gandhi if he would stay and help them fight for their rights. He agreed to stay.

The Struggle Begins

The bill to deny Indians the right to vote was close to passing when Gandhi went to work. He sent telegrams to political leaders. He also organized a petition drive against the bill.

The bill passed despite Gandhi's efforts. Yet Gandhi's example had energized the Indian people to fight for their rights. To assist them, Gandhi helped organize the Natal Indian Congress. This organization would monitor issues of importance to Indian people in South Africa. The Natal Indian Congress was much like India's Indian National Congress. That group expressed the concerns of Indians to the British government.

With the Natal Indian Congress in place, Gandhi turned to personal matters. In mid-1896, he returned to India. He was reunited with Kasturba and their two sons. Gandhi spent several months in India exposing the struggle in South Africa. He even wrote a pamphlet that talked about how badly Europeans treated Indians there. In late 1896, the Gandhi family traveled by ship back to South Africa.

When the ship arrived in South Africa, officials placed it under quarantine. Officials said they believed there was disease aboard. But many people believed the South African government didn't want Gandhi to come back. After three weeks, officials let the ship's passengers disembark. But Gandhi feared there would be more trouble, so he sent his family off the ship ahead of him.

Gandhi's suspicions were confirmed. Shortly after leaving the ship, a mob of angry Europeans attacked him. Fortunately, the wife of the local police superintendent helped him. The attack angered many people. They wanted Gandhi to press charges against his attackers, but Gandhi refused. He said he would not rely on the courts to fix other people's behavior.

Gandhi, in front of a microphone, delivers a prayer for peace in India.

New Way of Life

Gandhi had long believed in the importance of being self-reliant. He felt self-reliance would help Indians in their fight for equal rights. And Gandhi had taken the first steps with his own life.

Rather than sending out his shirts and collars to a laundry service, he learned how to wash, starch, and iron them himself. When an English barber refused to cut his hair, he learned how to cut it himself. Sometimes Gandhi failed miserably. His shirt collars wilted, and his hair was a mess. He refused to let the teasing that followed bother him. The important thing was he had done it himself. Eventually, Gandhi turned his back on European clothes. He wore simple cotton Indian-style clothes instead.

Gandhi expected everyone in his family and in his law office to be self-reliant, too. That included emptying and cleaning chamber pots. Kasturba rebelled at being asked to do this. Back in India, untouchables had done that kind of work.

Mohandas Gandhi

Gandhi visits England in 1931 to attend a conference on Indian constitutional reform.

Gandhi disliked the idea of forcing untouchables alone to do dirty work. He thought the entire caste system was too much like the racism he'd seen in South Africa. In his household, there would be no social classes. Kasturba and Gandhi fought over the issue. Eventually, Kasturba took her turn at emptying and cleaning the chamber pots. So did everyone else.

As time passed, Gandhi's efforts at self-reliance became even more extreme. He read books about medicine and herbs and acted as his family's doctor. He delivered his fourth son all by himself. When the pneumonic plague broke out in the Indian section of Johannesburg, Gandhi nursed the sickest patients without fear of catching the disease himself.

Gandhi also pulled his sons out of the local school. He didn't approve of the schools, which taught only in English. He didn't want his sons to know only European culture. Gandhi planned to teach them himself at home. However, he never had the time. So his four sons grew up without a decent education.

Betrayal

In 1899, the Boers in South Africa rebelled against the British government. The Boers were Dutch settlers. They wanted their own nation, free from British rule. The rebellion began the Boer War.

Gandhi felt that, if he wanted the rights that came with being a British citizen, he had to support the British. But he still didn't believe in using violence. Instead, he organized a group of Indians to provide medical care to the wounded during the war.

After the war, Gandhi and his family returned to India. He traveled the country to learn more about the Indian people. He talked to them about the problems Indians in South Africa faced. He met with the Indian National Congress. He left his family in India and headed back to Durban.

In Durban, Gandhi founded a newspaper called the *Indian Opinion*. The *Indian Opinion* was published in English and three Indian languages. It kept readers informed of the political situation in South Africa. It also encouraged them to improve their diets and sanitation habits. Gandhi believed the British would never take the Indians seriously as long as they lived in unsanitary conditions.

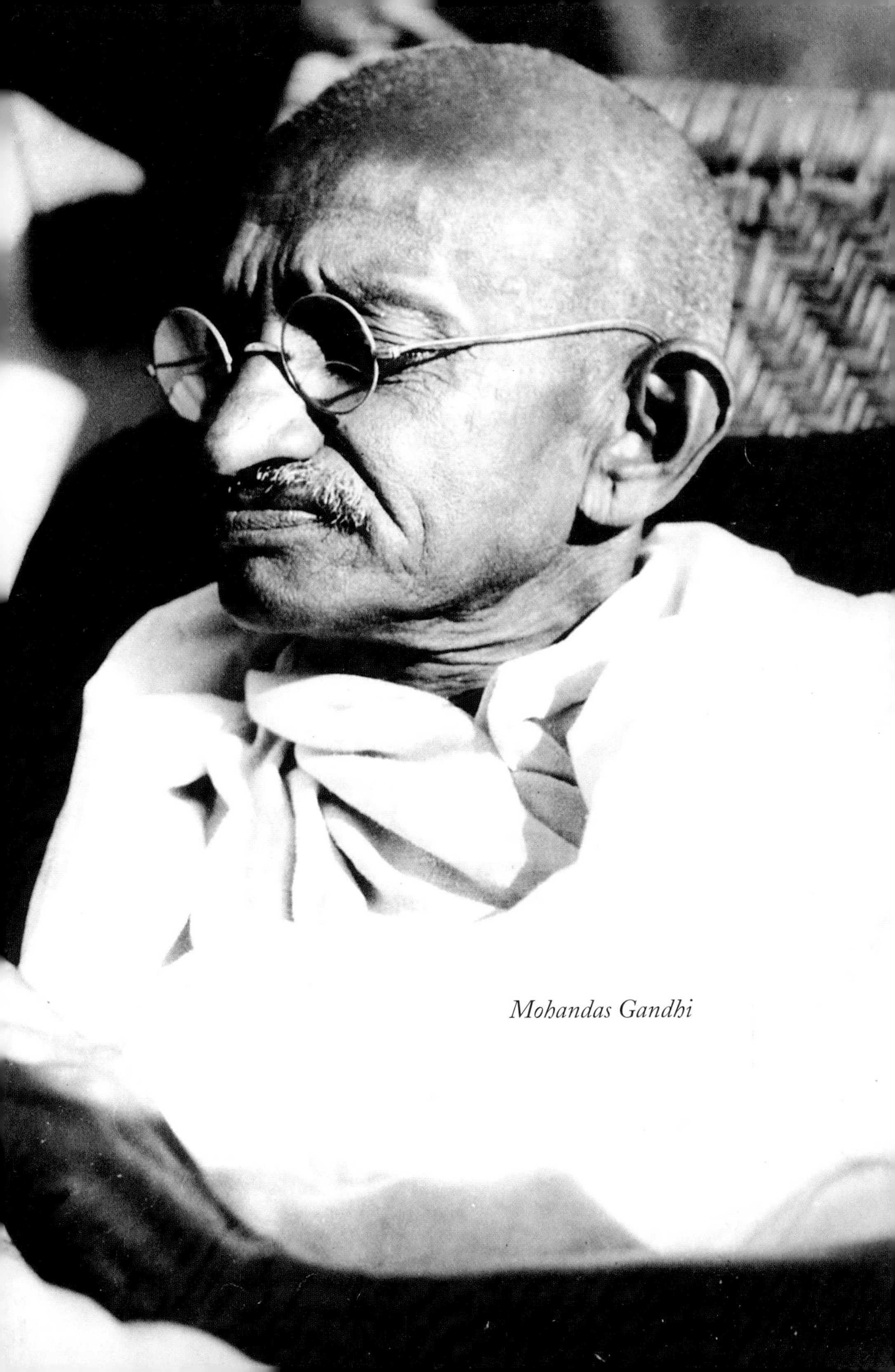

Mohandas Gandhi

Gandhi was inspired to try something new when he returned to South Africa. He bought a 90-acre (36-ha) farm and relocated the *Indian Opinion* there. He worked to make the farm a model of simple living. In 1905, Kasturba and his three youngest sons joined him there.

The British government had given Gandhi a medal for his work during the Boer War. He had hoped the British would treat Indians better since they had supported the British during the war. He was wrong.

In 1906, the government of Transvaal province in South Africa proposed a new law. It would require all Indians to register with the government. They would have to be fingerprinted. And they'd have to carry a permit with them at all times.

Gandhi and other Indians refused to accept this law. They called it the Black Act. And they began to think up ways to fight it. Gandhi suggested that Indians refuse to comply with the law. They wouldn't fight back violently. But they wouldn't cooperate.

Many Indians did refuse to cooperate. Police arrested them and sent them to jail. When the government realized they couldn't jail every Indian, they reconsidered. They said they would repeal the law if all Indians would register voluntarily. Gandhi agreed.

Mohandas Gandhi

One of Gandhi's mottos was, "Live simply, so that others may simply live."

The government did not keep its word, however. Government officials decided to enforce the law after all. In 1913, the law was amended to refuse recognition of any marriage that had not been performed as a Christian ceremony. That meant Hindu couples would not be considered married.

To fight this, Gandhi staged a protest. He and 3,000 other Indians burned their permits. The event marked one of many protests Gandhi organized. For nearly seven years, he led protest marches and spoke with British authorities in England about the problem. He also supported Indian workers in strikes. He, Kasturba, and thousands of others were arrested and jailed.

In June 1914, Gandhi and his followers realized some success in the South African Parliament. The parliament passed the Indian Relief Bill. It was key legislation in the struggle for Indians' equal rights. Later that year, a Nobel prize-winning Indian author gave Gandhi the title Mahatma, or Great Soul.

India Again

After a trip to England, Kasturba and Gandhi returned to India in 1915. There, Gandhi was welcomed as the Mahatma. Many Indians believed he could lead them to independence, as he had led Indians in South Africa to their freedom. For the first year after his return, Gandhi traveled around the country. He wore a traditional Indian turban and loincloth. He wore those simple clothes from that point on.

Indians had been seeking freedom from the British Empire for years. Indian leaders were asking Britain for home rule. So the Indian National Congress slowly had been trying to get more upper-class Indians into positions of power. Gandhi believed Indian independence had to be for all Indians. It should not be limited to the wealthy and educated.

Gandhi also believed that independence could only be won if all Indians worked together. But this was difficult. Indians were automatically divided at birth by the caste system. And although most Indians were Hindu, some were Muslim. The two groups had fought for years. Many Muslims wanted to secede from India and form a Muslim nation.

Mohandas Gandhi

Gandhi and his wife Kasturba

Gandhi began his quest for peace by setting an example. He began an ashram, or religious retreat, where he and his followers would live simply. He called it Satyagraha Ashram. Everyone who lived there had to promise to live by certain principles. They had to accept people of all classes and castes. They also had to be nonviolent and self-reliant.

Gandhi continued his pursuit of self-reliance. He learned to make his own thread using a spinning wheel. That thread then was woven into simple cloth. He encouraged all Indians to learn how to spin and weave. That way, they wouldn't have to rely on cloth from Great Britain.

Gandhi was living by example. But even with his success, Gandhi continued to be a controversial figure. He still supported the British government, even though he wanted independence for India. His dislike of the caste system also upset many Indians. But Gandhi continued his work, despite the criticism.

He began working outside of the ashram in 1917. He heard about a far away group of peasant farmers who were having trouble with British landowners. He represented the farmers in a court case and won. In 1918, he pledged to avoid eating until a textile workers' strike was settled. It was the first time he fasted for reform purposes. He would fast many times to get people to solve their differences.

Mohandas Gandhi

Meanwhile, he and other Indians waited for World War I to end. The British secretary of state for India had promised them that India would gain independence when the war ended. Instead, the opposite happened.

After the war, the British government extended rules that had limited the rights of Indians. Gandhi and thousands of Indians resisted with protests and non-cooperation. Some Indians protested by rioting. But Gandhi quickly spoke out against this violence. He began to wonder if the people of India understood satyagraha enough to practice it.

The British also responded to the rioting. In the province of Punjab, British soldiers opened fire on a group of Indian protesters. They killed nearly 400 and wounded more than 1,100. These deaths shocked Gandhi.

Gandhi and other Indian leaders realized Britain would not give up India without a fight. Gandhi's challenge now would be to see that the fight for independence was a peaceful one.

The March to Freedom

Following the massacre in Punjab, Gandhi called on Indians to support a new campaign. They were to boycott all British goods and avoid cooperating with British rules. Many Indians took up this cause. They refused to buy things made in Britain. They refused to go to British schools or British courts. They also stopped working for British employers. They refused to pay taxes to the British government.

Gandhi had hoped his movement would win independence in one year. When it did not, many Indian leaders called for violence. Gandhi resisted and urged peaceful protest. The Indian National Congress agreed with Gandhi. And the campaign for freedom continued.

In March 1922, the British authorities arrested Gandhi and charged him with sedition. Gandhi offered no defense. The court sentenced him to six years in prison. While in prison, Gandhi had surgery for appendicitis. But his incision didn't heal properly. Gandhi was freed after less than two years because officials were worried about public anger if he died.

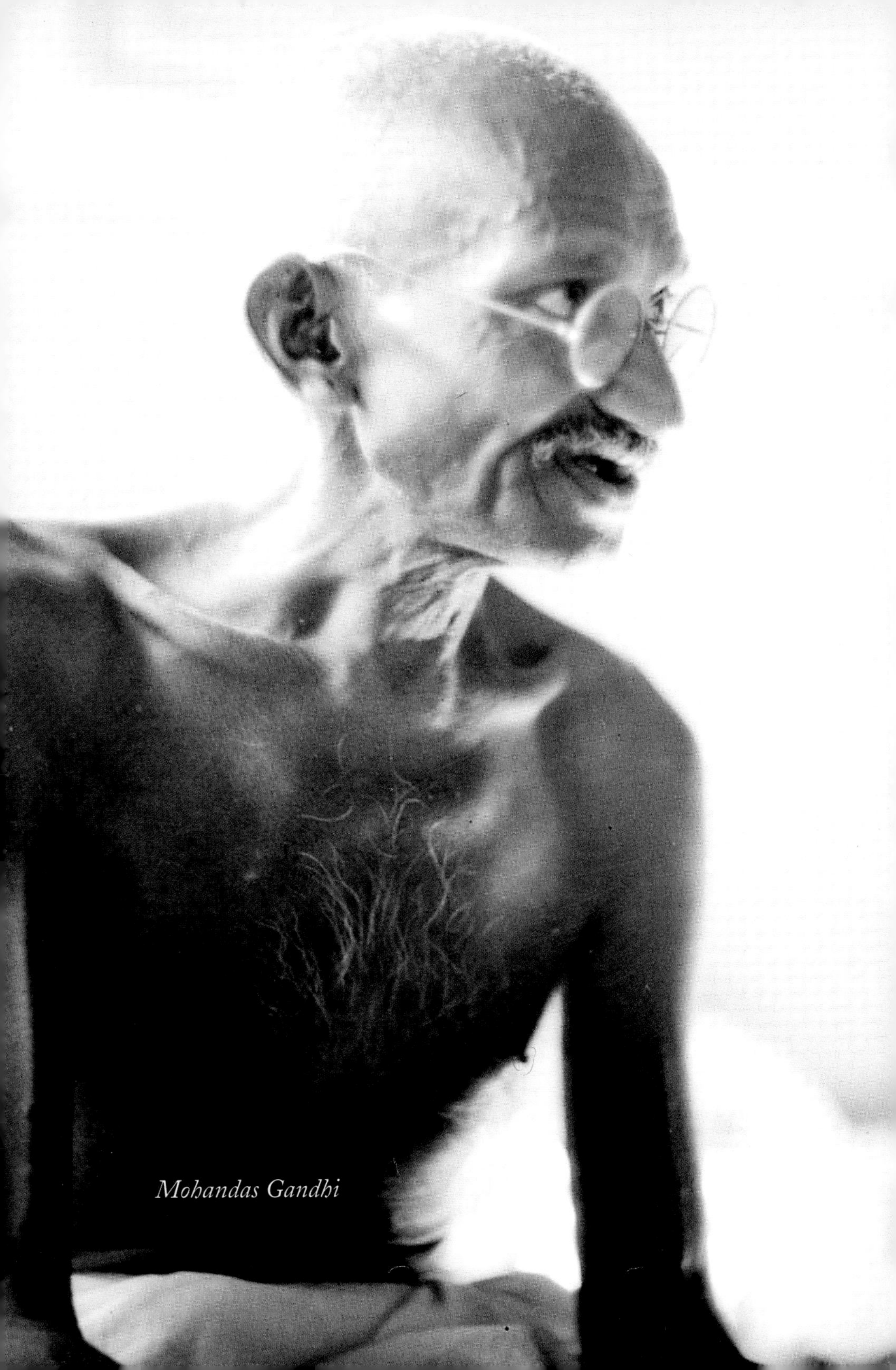

Mohandas Gandhi

The non-cooperation movement slowed while Gandhi was in prison. He worked to energize it again when he was released. He edited two magazines that urged resistance against the British government. He also encouraged Hindus and Muslims to work together for independence. He even fasted again to urge the two religions to put their differences aside.

By December 1928, many Indian leaders had lost their patience. The Indian National Congress called for full independence for India. It also called for a new campaign of civil disobedience. Shortly after that, Gandhi met with the viceroy of India to discuss the suffering and injustices faced by the Indian people.

One of the many injustices faced by Indians was the salt tax. Indians had to buy all their salt from Britain and pay an annual salt tax. The tax was equal to three days' work for most peasants. The viceroy ignored Gandhi's complaint about the salt tax being unfair. Gandhi then announced he would march to the sea.

Mohandas Gandhi

Gandhi visiting London in 1931.

On March 11, the 61-year-old Mahatma began the 240-mile (386-km) march to the coast. Several thousand Indians joined him along the way. When they arrived at the ocean, Gandhi began collecting sea salt from the shore. Almost immediately, Indians around the nation began collecting salt as well.

But it was a violation of British law to possess salt not purchased from Britain. The British police began arresting the Indians. The police began to beat Gandhi and the others while trying to break up the protest. The protesters refused to retaliate by hitting back. Eventually, the police arrested them and took them to jail. Gandhi was arrested along with some 60,000 Indians.

The British eventually freed Gandhi and the other protesters. Gandhi then began a string of meetings with British officials. The charismatic, often smiling leader even traveled to London to meet with top British officials. His words seemed to fall on deaf ears, however. He was back in prison in India a short while later.

As always, Gandhi used his time in prison to work on the cause. He wrote, prayed, and read. After spending so many years in prison, he was as comfortable behind bars as he was outside of them. Gandhi even said he enjoyed his isolation. It gave him time to reflect and plan.

Troubles Within

Gandhi's next campaign focused on the Indian people themselves. He wanted to eliminate the caste system that discriminated against so many people. He renamed the untouchables *Harijans*, or Children of God. He helped them learn about health and sanitation. And he began to demand better treatment for them from other Indians.

The Indian people resisted. They had lived with the caste system for hundreds of years. Why should they change it now, they asked. To make matters worse, the British were proposing a separate state for the untouchables. This was in direct opposition to Gandhi's dream of a united India. In September 1932, he vowed to fast to his death if the British proposal passed.

Gandhi's threat frightened many Indians. They scrambled to find an alternative to the British plan. They proposed a solution to Gandhi. The Indian solution gave the untouchables more representation in India's government and allowed them to vote with the other Hindus.

Gandhi sits cross-legged as he tries to settle a Congress Party dispute in Calcutta, India, in 1934.

Meanwhile, other Indians voted to allow untouchables into temples. That had never happened before. Hindus also dined with untouchables and allowed them in classes at the universities. Weakened and near death, Gandhi broke his fast.

Independence continued to elude India through the 1930s. In 1939, Great Britain was pulled into World War II. Gandhi supported the British in their fight against Nazi Germany. But he gave them only moral support. He didn't help recruit soldiers or medical workers as he had in past British conflicts. Some Indian leaders proposed a deal with Britain. They would help with the war in exchange for independence. But British officials refused the proposal.

In June 1942, Gandhi urged further non-cooperation among the Indian people. He was jailed and was still in jail in 1944 when Kasturba died. She had been his wife for 62 years. Despite his loss, Gandhi continued working. He and other Indian leaders were released a few months later. Yet independence for India remained an elusive goal.

Self-government was granted to India following the end of World War II. But Britain still had control. Now the problem was within India itself. Muslim leaders were still calling for a separate country. A British commission tried to find a compromise. Their suggestion resulted in rioting and bloodshed between Muslims and Hindus throughout India. Gandhi said more than 10,000 Muslims and Hindus died in the fighting.

"My present mission is the most difficult and complicated one of my life," he said. "Hindus and Muslims should learn to live together in peace and amity. Otherwise I should die in the attempt." Gandhi did not realize that his words of sadness were also a prophecy.

Mohandas Gandhi

The Light Goes Out

The British Empire granted independence to India on August 15, 1947. But for Gandhi, it was an incomplete victory. Religious differences divided the country. India was divided into India and Pakistan. Hindus living in Pakistan and Muslims living in India found themselves victims of violence. Rioting and killing began again.

Gandhi could not stand by while such violence raged. He traveled to Calcutta and fasted to urge Hindus and Muslims to end the violence. Miraculously, they did. Indians still respected the Mahatma. Gandhi had the same effect in other cities he visited. But he could not be everywhere. In some places, fighting continued.

In January 1948, Gandhi began another fast. He refused both food and water. His body began to weaken, and doctors feared his kidneys were close to failing. Dr. Rajendra Prasad, the new president of India's congress, worked feverishly to get cooperation from the groups that were fighting.

The sun sets behind a sculpture of Gandhi in Calcutta, India.

Prasad and other leaders met with Gandhi to convince him that the plan would work. Gandhi could break his fast, they said. Gandhi did so reluctantly. Gandhi was very weak from fasting. He had to be carried everywhere, even to prayers.

Two days after he broke his fast, he was at a meeting when he heard a blast. It was a bomb thrown by a young Hindu refugee. The young man had seen many Hindus harmed by Muslims. And he blamed Gandhi for the violence. Gandhi said people should pity the young man, not hate him.

The bombing incident inspired another man. Nathuram Godse was the editor of a weekly Hindu newspaper. He, too, was angry about the creation of Pakistan. In the late afternoon of January 30, 1948, he went to where Gandhi was praying in New Delhi, India.

As the frail Mahatma was helped to the place where he would pray, Godse pulled a handgun out of his pocket. He shot Gandhi three times. The smile faded from Gandhi's face and he died with a whispered Rama. Rama is the Hindu word for God.

Later that evening, Indian Prime Minister Jawaharlal Nehru spoke about Gandhi. He told a shocked nation, "The light has gone out of our lives."

The body of Mohandas Gandhi was covered with rose petals and carried to the site of his cremation in New Delhi, India, on January 31, 1948.

Gandhi was cremated in a traditional Hindu ceremony. While his body was no more, his spirit has lived on in the hearts of millions of people who believe justice is possible without violence.

Timeline

October 2, 1869: Mohandas Karamchand Gandhi is born in Porbandar, India.

1883: Gandhi marries Kasturba.

1888: Gandhi sails to London, England, to study law.

1891: Gandhi passes the bar exam, and returns to India to practice law.

1893: Gandhi moves to South Africa to join an Indian law firm.

1894: Gandhi organizes the Natal Indian Congress.

1914: South Africa passes the Indian Relief Bill.

1916: Back in India, Gandhi establishes Satyagraha Ashram.

1922: Gandhi is arrested by British police for sedition.

1930: Gandhi sets out on the historic salt march.

1932: Gandhi begins a "fast unto death" to protest segregation of the untouchables.

1947: India is granted independence.

January 30, 1948: Gandhi is assassinated by a Hindu fanatic.

Web Sites

Would you like to learn more about Gandhi? Please visit **www.abdopub.com** to find up-to-date Web site links about Gandhi and the country of India. These links are routinely monitored and updated to provide the most current information available.

Mohandas Gandhi

Glossary

boycott

To refrain from having any dealings with something, such as to refuse to buy anything produced by a particular company.

Buddhism

A religion of eastern and central Asia.

caste

A division of Indian society based on heredity.

chamber pot

A large bowl used in place of a toilet.

discrimination

To treat some people better or worse than others because of their race, religion, gender, or some other factor.

Hindu

A person who believes a body of religious beliefs and practices native to India.

Muslim

A person who practices the religion of Islam.

quarantine

To restrict the movement of people to stop the spread of disease.

racism

A belief that people of some races are better than those of other races.

secede

To withdraw from an organized body, such as a nation.

sedition

Causing discontent with a government.

segregation

When races are kept separate from one another.

viceroy

The governor of a country who rules as a representative of the ruling nation.

Index